Mariposa Sources, LLC
info@mariposasources.com

Living Your Best life with the 5 F's

Faith; Family; Fun; Fitness; Finance

Dedication

This book goes out to everyone who tended to the soil, planted seeds, watered the field, gave sunlight to the crops or were even part of the pruning process. I needed all of you to become who I am today.

To Zulma:

My Lobster! I was made to love you and will enjoy doing so for the rest of my life! I'm grateful to share this life with you as we raise our children together.

To My Boys (Julian, Luca, and Mateo):

You are my biggest whys and I hope you guys know by now there isn't anything that I won't do for you! The main reason I want more in life isn't for me, it's for what I could do for you!

To Jacinta:

My amazing daughter! You don't know how much you have motivated me to be the kind of Dad that I am. I'm grateful for every moment and cherish the ability to have shared time with loved ones.

To Mom and Dad:

Without you there's no me! Thank you for everything you've done and do to help me maximize my potential. I hope to make you proud!

Table of Contents

Introduction

This book is designed to help you take immediate, massive action towards living your best life by breaking down the key categories that I believe complete an amazing life!

If you allow it to, this guide will navigate you out of your comfort zone and into being comfortable with uncomfortable situations.

The first day of your new journey starts now; start creating new habits that reflect the future you.

Starting with…

Faith

This competency is the greatest of all and the foundation of everything that you stand on and aspire to be. It's like the navigational system for your soul. This area will be shaped by your experiences and environment, so it is vital to be in tune with yourself.

Believing in something you cannot physically see, touch, or feel can be challenging, to say the least. Yet, it is one of the most vital competencies of all.

Being intelligent creatures of energy, we obtain the greatest control over our outcomes when thoughts and emotions combine. It is in those moments that we often feel belief or disbelief. Those attributes will increase or decrease in relation to yourself, someone else or something else. Either way, there is a strong emotional connection tied to the expected outcome or results.

The goal is to learn to be present and operate in a state of gratitude.

Thankful for where I have been, where I am, and where I am going. When you know you have a purpose way bigger than just yourself, you understand that it requires you to be the very best version that you can produce every single day. It will become a habit that you'll absolutely be OBSESSED with!

Family

Family is everything! Family is not just the tight core of relatives and friends you hold close, but also the extended group of individuals who share your ideals and respect your intentions. 'Tight core' describes the individuals you hold the closest to your heart and allow to be an intricate part of your life.

This group will fuel your 'whys' and support you in life. Your 'why' is the emotional connection and/or reason that inspires you to do what you do. However different each relationship is, the common factors of love and respect will always be the defining characteristics of the group of relationships.

Understanding that everyone's journey is unique and learning how to "allow" certain situations, compared to feeling the need to agree or disagree with someone will be key. It's important to allow certain situations because the situation is tied to someone else's journey as well and they might not be of the same mindset. Allowing is also giving someone the time and/or opportunity to be them without trying to change their actioning or outlook. Even though their actions or way of thinking might not be your cup of tea. Learning to expand your level of patience and understanding will increase your ability to apply this principle.

The purpose of allowing is important because it helps you avoid absorbing negative energy. Negative energy could affect your ability to make decisions in a positive light, which could lead to unfortunate interactions and/or disagreements.

The goal is for each of us to teach and share these concepts early to the ones we love. Finding a way to share things learned by life experience while remembering to use the lens of the person you are engaging with is the major component that increases the potential for a positive outcome.

Staying in the moment while seeking understanding is the best way to have dialogue conducive for favorable outcomes. When you stay in the moment, you will discover that there is respect, understanding, caring and empathy present as well.

Create good habits.

Add professionalism to your family structure and treat it like a business. Creating schedules for the family needs does help with organization and effectiveness, or having a family meeting to discuss vacation options will go a long way with relationship building and improve effectiveness in communication.

When it comes to how we treat family, many times it's easier to take a loved one's efforts for granted compared to those of a colleague. It is imperative to make a conscious effort in fostering and developing a genuine relationship rather than assuming what their opinions and thoughts may be, which can lead to you taking them for granted.

Being open and honest, with love and respect, while communicating and following through with commitments will establish the trust needed to see past the tangible, in order to build and manifest.
Pair these concepts with patience and understanding and you have the ingredients necessary for true partnership.

When Zulma and I had our first son, Julian, we noticed there would be times where she didn't feel like her normal self, even her dreams were different. That open communication and trust led to us finding out about postpartum depression, which allowed us to get the tools and support needed for our family. Because love was at the forefront, with communication and commitment, we were able to move past a situation that could have been crippling to say the least.

People believe what they see and that is why it is very important that you demonstrate behavior that does not contradict the things you speak about. Being consistent creates a moral authority, and that is huge when trying to inspire a sense of accountability, along with the ability to earn trust.

Fun

Taking the time to celebrate wins is monumental self-care critical for progress. It creates paradigm changes along with motivation for future endeavors.

Having the work you have done feel "worth it" is a natural craving that isn't always satisfied. Sometimes you have to intentionally smell the roses to remind yourself how far you have come. This will provide a feeling of satisfaction, as it confirms the actions leading to that moment were well worth it. This is a time when you get to live and focus on the present, while developing aspirations for the future.

Be sure to include your family in the celebration of wins. Remember how fortunate you are to have the circle that you do and appreciate the value they offer to your life. Find fun and creative ways to deepen the bonds by sharing dreams and making tangible goals happen together to develop lasting and meaningful relationships.

Learning how to attach the feeling you get from a reward or gift to your journey and/or current process is a complete game changer. For example, let's say you're going to the gym to increase the attractiveness of your appearance. That can take an amount of time that could be discouraging to you. But, telling yourself how good it feels to commit to your goals and believing in the process will aid in keeping you in a positive mindset and motivated to do the actions required that will derive the desired results.

Not being thirsty for just results but being hungry for the work will be the day you retire your mind from the conundrum you're stuck in. This will put you on the path of a fruitful and ever so rewarding journey.

Embracing your journey is when the concept of living your best life starts to become real. You'll notice an increase in morale and confidence, as you put more effort into guarding the quality of your life and experiences. They will greatly affect the consistency of your habits in a positive manner, and you will experience the elements around you starting to follow suit as well.

Fitness

It is extremely hard to take the mind where the body won't follow. Being creatures of habits and feelings, having a body that is healthy with a strong physiology is imperative for consistency and growth.

Fitness does wonders for creating consistent habits and the best one of all is discipline. One of the first things you will need to get used to is scheduling or 'time management'. 'Time management' is the process of organizing and planning how to allocate your time between different tasks and activities. Scheduling allows you to work smarter, not harder, leading to greater productivity and reduced stress. Developing your time management skills along with the ability to create and set goals will be paramount to your success. Also, working out can be uncomfortable and difficult at times and learning how to thrive under those conditions improves your overall chances for success.

Learning to enjoy work with delayed gratification is the key to trusting the process and staying consistent. The body is a very complex structure and the competencies, like managing change, interpersonal awareness and analytical thinking, are needed in order to have it operating in prime condition. This is similar to what is required for the soul, spirit and mind to develop fully.

Being around like-minded people harnessing the same energy is beyond big, this aids with your development and helps solidify situations. You want shared experiences and the opportunity to learn from their previous experiences. This could be as simple as remembering to have a growth mindset. Being a part of a community provides inspiration and motivation while fostering accountability.

Understanding that diet is more than food choices. Paying attention to what you put into your body (food, energy, people).

Finance

Money is something we need to survive and live, so it's smart to get educated about it. Financial literacy is important to understand how to effectively and efficiently keep everything together. If there are money woes, the mind and body tend to follow suit if not mitigated.

Create a budget that includes all your monthly expenses in order to compare them with your income. You want to have lines to record and account for any variances, i.e. look at where you can lower your expenses. Since most life events are tied to finances, having this area operating correctly will add, improve and sustain a certain level of comfort in every aspect of your life due to the planning, structure and available means.

Share ideas with your circle and collaborate. Experience diverse ways to engage, celebrate and connect. Growing a sense of community with planning is essential to creating legacy and generational increases. So going on vacations and celebrating holidays are all methodical processes that will create a strong and sound culture which will harvest a bountiful and rich future together. Planning holiday activities like dinners, coordinating travel and attending life events all take time, communication, and helps shape bonds when done together is a positive light.

Create a schedule to do regular study, research and follow upon any spending/saving trends to measure and track your progress. If there are any deficits, set specific goals and create a detailed plan that shows how you expect to improve metrics by the next review.

Establishing a rewards and consequences system will encourage effort and focus while deepening the commitment and accountability.

Resolution

The glue in your tool-belt that brings it all together!

Mental Toughness and Emotional Intelligence are what brings these 5 F's (Faith, Family, Fun, Fitness and Finance) all together. See them like filters and lenses to a camera. Think about how they are able to adjust the focus in order to better view the desired object. Observe how they zoom in or out to have everything they need in the frame of a beautiful photograph while also having the ability to blur out the undesired objects. The ability to focus on what is important is the key to prioritization. The person with their priorities in order is a person with their life in order.

Perception and paradigm are the key to Mental Toughness and Emotional Intelligence. Together, they aid you in the pursuit of focusing on the right things, at the right time, in the right way.

How you see things is how you will most likely react to it, so learning how to see people, situations or even challenges with favorable intentions will increase your chances of receiving favorable results.

Final Note

Just like tension and resistance are key components to building muscle and strength due to working out, causing the micro-tears in the muscle fibers needed for growth; our mind requires similar stimulation in order to foster growth.

In other words, if your body physically needs the challenge of stress in order to grow, then your mind needs to experience a measure of difficulty, challenges and/or tough situations in order to develop mentally as well. This creates 'resilience', the capacity to withstand or to recover quickly from difficulties.

Staying present while continuously controlling what you can is required to grow.

When you comprehend and control your own thoughts and emotions regarding the elements or people around you, that is when you know you are *'Living Your Best Life'*

About the Author

A lover of life and people, Vincent learned at an early age to embrace opportunities that connect with the community. Raised in Pomona California in a time when music and sports programs were abundant, Vincent was placed on a path to find his purpose and develop his gifts.

Now, rather it is keeping a beat for a performance ensemble, leading a team or individual to accomplish their goals or creating content for his favorite brands, Vincent's ability to motivate and inspire people is the gift that he is most appreciative for and that is why he has chosen to write his first book; making his experiences and unique concepts available to benefit anyone who can use them.